KAKURO
AND OTHER
NUMBER P...

Compiled by
Kjartan Poskitt
Illustrated by Philip Reeve

SCHOLASTIC INC.

New York   Toronto   London   Auckland   Sydney
Mexico City   New Delhi   Hong Kong   Buenos Aires

To my granny Margaret Fenton age 100. If this was a book of crossword puzzles, she'd finish it in 20 minutes.

ISBN 0-439-88051-3

Text and Kjarposko puzzles copyright © 2006 by Kjartan Poskitt
Su Doku, Kakuro, and Bridge puzzles copyright © 2006 by Puzzle Media
Illustrations copyright © 2000-2005 by Philip Reeve

All rights reserved. Published by Scholastic Inc., 557 Broadway, New York, NY 10012, by arrangement with Scholastic Ltd.

12 11 10 9 8 7 6 5 4 3 2   6 7 8 9 10 11/0

Printed in the U.S.A.   40
First Scholastic U.S.A. printing, May 2006

CONTENTS

Introduction

A few weeks ago the headquarters of the Murderous Math Organization was a scary place to be. It was long past midnight and all was deathly quiet. You'd be forgiven for thinking that the place was empty, but it wasn't! All the lights were shining bright, and everybody was frantically scribbling away on anything they could find including scraps of paper, old $5 bills, pizza boxes ... they were even scribbling on the pizzas themselves, but why?

The answer was SU DOKU puzzles. The Organization had already produced their own highly-acclaimed-international-best-selling-exquisitely-detailed-lavishly-produced-no-pages-missing-reasonably-priced-handy-for-the-bathroom Su Doku book, but in doing so the puzzles had completely taken over everybody's brains. Everyone in the Organization from the grand editor right down to the lowly rubber-plant waterer was sitting in dead silence trying to fit numbers into Su Doku grids, and covering the place with little notes and plans to help them. But as soon as one grid was completed and defeated, two more would rise up and take its place. As everyone battled valiantly to overcome the never-ending* swarm of Su Dokus, the telephones went unanswered, coffee was left undrunk, the grand editor's nails were unpainted, the rubber plant was unwatered, and the entire might of the Organization ground to a halt.

It seemed that nothing could break the addictive curse of the Su Doku until one morning a different puzzle arrived. It was to be the savior of the Organization and it might even save the world as we know it.

The new puzzle was KAKURO. It's kind of like Su Doku because you fill numbers into a grid, but the difference is that as well as exercising your logic skills, you can use use your arithmetic skills too. There's just one danger with Kakuros. They are so much fun that we're worried the entire world might end up doing them instead. So although we're going to give you a load of cool Kakuros to try in this book, you'll also find some other puzzles too. And, of course, just in case you're getting withdrawal symptoms, we've put in a few Su Dokus just for old times' sake.

(*Actually, if you've read our Su Doku book you'll know there are only **6,670,903,752,021,072, 936,960** possible Su Doku grids, but that's still quite a few to get through.)

Kakuro

Here's a very simple Kakuro puzzle. The idea is to fill every empty box with a number between 1 and 9.

Look at the square marked $_4\backslash^9$. This means that the digits in the boxes underneath it must add up to 4. *These digits have to be different.*

Also the digits in the boxes to the right must add up to 9, and they must be different too. The other numbered boxes also indicate what their rows and columns must add up to.

Here's the puzzle again, but we'll throw in a few letters to make it easier to describe what we're talking about.

We know boxes a+b= 4. We also know that b+e = 3.

Here's where the tricky part starts. If you have two digits that add up to 4 *and they have to be different*, then the digits must be 1+3. Two digits adding up to 3 must be 1+2.

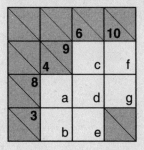

As the number in box b is needed for both the 3 and the 4, then box b must be 1. Immediately you can see that a=3 and e = 2.

Let's see how far we've gotten:

Now look at the 8, which is telling us that $3 + d + g = 8$.

There are two ways to make 8 from three different digits: $1+2+5$ or $1+3+4$. We already have a 3 in place, so the digits for d and g must be 1 and 4, but which is which?

Look at the number 6 on the top row. It's telling us that $c + d + 2 = 6$. If d was 4 then c would have to be 0, which is not allowed. Therefore $d = 1$ and that means $c = 3$. Almost finished! There are only boxes f and g left to fill in, and by now the answers should be obvious:

(If these last answers are *not* obvious to you, don't worry. Just abandon all hope of ever doing Kakuros and instead use this as a coloring book. There's no shame in it. In fact a lot of people who are addicted to Kakuros wish they'd just stuck to coloring in the first place.)

TRICKS

THE EXTRA BOX

Here's part of a bigger puzzle. Without filling in any other numbers, you can tell what should go in box a !

Look at the three numbers 12, 6, and 8 on the top. They tell us that all the boxes marked x together add up to 12+6+8 = 26.

Now look at the rows going across. All the boxes marked x PLUS the box marked a add up to 10+11+12 = 33. Since 33 is 7 more than 26, this means a=7.

WHICH IS WHICH

Here's another piece of a puzzle. You can tell what x is without solving a, b, c or d!

Here you can see that a+b=3, so a must be either 1 or 2. Similarly, c+d=3, so c has to be 1 or 2 as well. But since a and c are in the same row, they can't be the same number, so one of them is 1 and the other is 2. We don't know which is which, but we do know that a+c=3. Therefore the 9 tells us that x has to be 6.

THE ONLY OPTION

Remember that you can only use the numbers 1-9 in the boxes, so can you tell what must go in box q ?

There are two ways to make 15 with two digits: 7+8 and 9+6. There are three ways to make 9 with three digits but none of them uses 7, 8, or 9. Therefore q must be 6.

HELPFUL NUMBERS

Some numbers make life easier. Suppose you have a row of three empty boxes with a 7 at the end. The three numbers have to be 1+2+4, so 7 is helpful. If you have three boxes with a 9 at the end, the numbers could be 1+3+5 or 2+3+4 or 1+2+6, so 9 is not so helpful. (Of course if you find one of the boxes has a 4 in it, then you know that the other two boxes have 2 and 3.) Here's a list of all the helpful numbers.

You'll see that the helpful numbers are only helpful when you have the right number of empty boxes. Although 29 is helpful with four empty boxes, if there are five empty boxes then there are *eight* different combinations that could go in!

You might want to fold down the corner of page 11 so you can keep flipping back to the chart. It's very helpful!

Number of empty boxes	Helpful number	Only possible digits
2	**3**	$1 + 2$
	4	$1 + 3$
	16	$7 + 9$
	17	$8 + 9$
3	**6**	$1 + 2 + 3$
	7	$1 + 2 + 4$
	23	$6 + 8 + 9$
	24	$7 + 8 + 9$
4	**10**	$1 + 2 + 3 + 4$
	11	$1 + 2 + 3 + 5$
	29	$5 + 7 + 8 + 9$
	30	$6 + 7 + 8 + 9$
5	**15**	$1 + 2 + 3 + 4 + 5$
	16	$1 + 2 + 3 + 4 + 6$
	34	$4 + 6 + 7 + 8 + 9$
	35	$5 + 6 + 7 + 8 + 9$

OUR EXPERT, TRUFFLES, WILL GIVE YOU A FEW TIPS TO GET STARTED. GOOD LUCK!

Dead Simple Puzzles

1

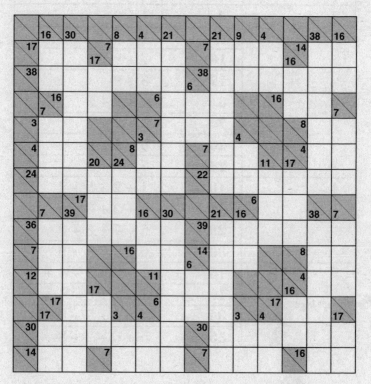

The first set of three boxes lying along the bottom line add up to 7, so they must contain 1,2, and 4. You cannot put 4 or 2 directly underneath the 4, therefore the box under the 4 must be 1. You can use this same trick SIX more times around the edges of this puzzle! Also you should be able to see that the top left corner and bottom right corner both have to be 9! Always look for corners where the pairs of boxes add to 16 and 17.

TRUFFLES' TIPS

2

The first empty box on the bottom line must be 1. It's just like the example on page 7. Always look for these corners where the pairs of boxes add up to 3 and 4. This puzzle has FOUR more of them! The 34 on the right-hand edge is helpful, the digits must be 4,6,7,8,9. The top digit must be the 4 since 4 is the only digit you can use to add up to the 7.

3

You can use the same tip I gave you for puzzle 1 three times in this puzzle. And by the way, 39 with six empty boxes is helpful! The numbers have to be 4+5+6+7+8+9.

4

Both 21 and 22 with six empty boxes
are helpful. 21=1+2+3+4+5+6 and
22=1+2+3+4+5+7

15

5

Kakuro puzzle grid with clue numbers: 23, 17, 23, 4, 29, 30, 16, 7, 3, 4 / 17, 13, 26, 6 / 11, 28, 27, 7, 29 / 29, 16, 10, 12, 37, 23 / 23, 4, 30, 29, 24, 16, 29 / 4, 23, 29, 24, 32 / 16, 16, 16, 30 / 8, 23, 22, 11, 14, 15, 3 / 29, 16, 4, 11, 33 / 27, 6, 25, 26, 6, 25 / 16, 17, 7, 23, 23, 17 / 4, 4, 4, 31, 3 / 3, 4, 7, 28, 23 / 6, 26, 16

TRUFFLES' TIPS

Don't forget that 29 with four empty boxes is helpful: 9+8+7+5. There are six of them here.

6

7

8

9

10

11

A Kakuro puzzle grid with clue numbers: 24, 23, 30, 17, 16, 30 across the top row; 17, 16, 17 in the second row; 17, 23 in the third; and various clues throughout the grid.

12

13

Watch out! This is very similar to
puzzle 12. You'll have to concentrate so
you won't get mixed up!

24

14

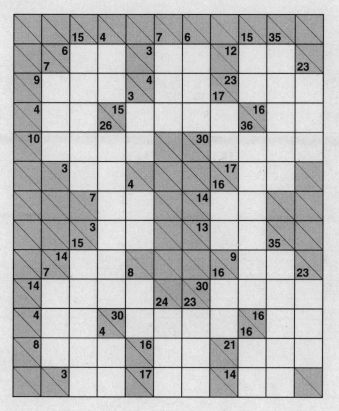

16

A Kakuro-style puzzle grid with the following clues: 3, 9, 24, 17 (top row); 3, 16, 38, 19; 7, 41, 10, 27; 16, 17, 4, 29, 29, 4; 8, 29, 17, 23, 29; 16, 14, 24; 24, 24; 23, 23, 23; 23, 17, 6; 20, 16, 8; 20, 6; 16, 26, 8; 16, 3; 30, 10; 14, 3.

Any row of eight empty boxes is helpful!
41 uses the numbers 1,2,3,5,6,7,8,9.
38 uses the numbers 1,2,3,4,5,6,8,9.
(Subtract the number you're trying to
make from 45 to find the digit you
don't need. E.g. 45-41=4. This means to
make 41 from 8 digits you use all the
digits 1-9 except 4.)

TRUFFLES' TIPS

19

20

Devious Puzzles

21

(Kakuro puzzle grid with the following clue numbers)

Across/Down clues as printed in the grid cells:

Row 1: 16, 26, 30, 17

Row 2: 16, 16, 40, 17, 37, 17

Row 3: 30, 17, 30, 16

Row 4: 17, 29, 29, 16, 10

Row 5: 38, 14, 4

Row 6: 24, 6

Row 7: 23, 11, 12, 17, 30, 7

Row 8: 42, 3, 3

Row 9: 4, 29, 3, 4, 17

Row 10: 10, 24

Row 11: 3, 16

Here's an easy start to our Devious
section! Remember to look for corners
where the pairs of boxes add up to
16 and 17. Don't forget that 30 with
four empty boxes is helpful: 9+8+7+6.
Also 40, 42, 37, and 38 with 8 empty
boxes are all helpful!

TRUFFLES' TIPS

22

23

24

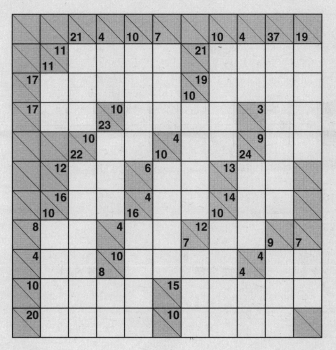

25

26

28

A Kakuro puzzle grid with the clue numbers as follows:

Top row clues (across headers): 4, 23, 30, 3, 35, 20, 3, 29, 33, 16

Left/down clues throughout the grid: 28, 26, 17, 4/7, 24, 16, 3, 10, 23/15, 9, 10, 7, 3, 7, 5, 9, 4, 4, 4, 3, 3, 4, 4/23, 35, 20, 30, 3, 7, 14/26, 7/17, 4/29, 9, 24, 11, 4/4, 23/3, 16/4, 16, 28, 26, 26, 28

29

A Kakuro puzzle grid with various clue numbers including: 23, 17, 28, 17, 17, 28, 26, 23, 16, 16, 13, 21, 14, 35, 23, 4, 23, 4, 7, 12, 23, 21, 18, 7, 12, 16, 22, 21, 17, 16, 22, 16, 35, 17, 24, 17, 26, 16, 33, 23, 19, 12, 14, 8, 28, 10, 14, 7, 4, 7, 37, 3, 15, 19, 7, 4, 7.

30

A Kakuro puzzle grid (puzzle number 30).

Drastic Puzzles

31

32

34

35

36

37

38

39

A Kakuro puzzle grid with the following clues:

Top row clue cells: 11, 10, 29, 35, 7, 30, 29

- 34, 21 (row clues)
- 27, 5, 12
- 6, 16, 16
- 8, 31, 15
- 7, 4, 14, 4, 24, 35
- 11, 13, 31, 17
- 8, 17, 25, 16, 16
- 14, 16, 4, 7, 30, 3
- 6, 3, 23, 11, 6
- 29, 15, 23, 3, 12
- 4, 8, 10
- 17, 21, 26

Bridges

This puzzle is perfect for artsy people because you don't have to put numbers in, you just draw straight lines.

The idea is to link all the numbered islands together using bridges. Here are the rules:

• The bridges must go horizontally or vertically and they cannot cross each other

• You can't have more than two bridges joining the same two islands. The number on each island says how many bridges must lead to it.

• All the islands must be linked up together.

Here's a VERY easy start!

② ③ ①

② ③ ①

You need to link up these six islands with the right number of bridges going to each island. But you can't do this...

... because you can't put more than two bridges between two islands. You can't do this either...

...because the two groups of islands are separate. Here is the only possible answer:

Where do the names KAKURO, SU DOKU, and BRIDGE come from?

Logic puzzles like Kakuro and Su Doku are especially popular in Japan, which is why the names have a Japanese sound.

KAKURO is an invented word that means cross sums. It's a shortened version of the words kasan (the Japanese word for addition) and kurosu (which sounds a bit like cross).

SU DOKU is short for "Suji wa dokushin ni kagiru," which is Japanese for "the numbers must be single."

The odd thing is that when the Japanese say "single" they also mean "unmarried," so it means that the numbers must be unmarried. Whether or not the numbers are allowed to share a pizza or go out to see a band together is not known.

Incidentally, the name for the BRIDGE puzzles comes from the English word "bridge," which means a bridge.

Now we'll experiment with a full Bridge puzzle and pick up a few tips.

(The letters don't appear on normal puzzles. These are just for our explanations.)

The first thing to look for is the island with the number 8. This has to have two bridges going off it in every direction, so we can draw two bridges going from this island to each of the islands marked w, x, y, and z.

Now look at the island marked 1a. Since the bridges have to be vertical or horizontal, 1a can only be linked to island 3b or 2c, but the island marked 2c is now blocked by the bridges between ⑧ and 2z. Therefore 1a must link with a single bridge to 3b.

So far these links are obvious and you can immediately tell if you have to put in one or two bridges. When things get tougher, sometimes it's important just to find out which islands are linked, even if you don't know if it's with one or two bridges. Try this:

THE DOTTED LINES TRICK!

Look at island 4d. It is between 2c and 2e, so you might think you could just link with two bridges to both of them. But if you do that, you can't join any more bridges onto the group and so these three would be separate from all the other islands. Since all the islands must be linked together, at least one bridge from 4d must go up to 3f. Since you don't know if it's one bridge or two bridges, mark this in with a dotted line to remind you to check later. This dotted line will also tell you that there cannot be a bridge between 2m and 1n.

It's always worth looking for islands with high numbers. If an island has a 7 or 8 on it, then it must connect to the islands in all four directions. If an island is at the edge of the puzzle with a 5 or 6 on it, then it must connect with at least one bridge in each of the three available directions. (For example, look at the island numbered 5 in our test puzzle. It has to have bridges going left, right, and downward.)

Can you complete our starting puzzle? The answer is at the end of the book.

Dead Simple Puzzles

1

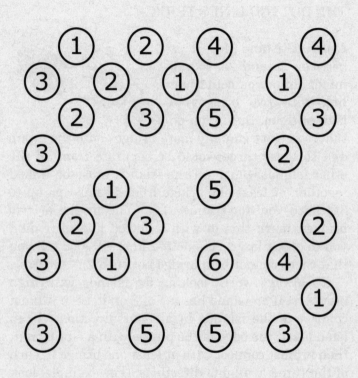

On the second row down, the two ① islands cannot be linked or they will be isolated. Each island only has one other island it can link to, so you can draw the bridges in! Now the ② on the second row cannot link to the ① directly below it or the three islands will be isolated, therefore the ② must link to the ③ at the end. On you go...

TRUFFLES' TIPS

Start by filling in all eight bridges from the ⑧ island, and also all six bridges from the ⑥ island!

3

Look at the ③ on the second row. There is only one way it can be linked with three bridges. After that, you know where the bridges linked to the ④ on the top row have to go.

4

5

10

19

The Su Doku Invasion

2005 was the year that Su Dokus invaded. At the start of the year hardly anybody had ever heard of them, and books, newspapers, and magazines were allowed to deliver facts and stories completely uncluttered by little numbered grids. But one day it all changed.

SORRY, BUT WE NOW INTERRUPT THIS BOOK TO BRING YOU AN URGENT NEWSFLASH!

"Nearly every printing machine in the world has been reprogrammed to zap us all with Su Doku puzzles."

Sure enough, Su Dokus suddenly started turning up everywhere! Even Shakespearean drama was infected...

Lady Scrabble
"Fie cos, what ails thee this bright morrow?"

Sir D'koo
"Why, 'tis this devilish riddle. Thou must place ye numbers 1-9 but once in every row, column, and even unto ye 3x3 blocks."

Lady Scrabble
"Oh, my."

Since you've probably already seen Su Dokus, we're not going to spend ages explaining them all here (you'll find everything you need to know in the book *Su Doku: 100 Fun Number Puzzles*), but in case you need a little help getting started, Truffles will give you a few tips.

Dead Simple Puzzles

1

		3		9				8
	5		4		1		3	6
		7		4	8		5	9
	9		3		7	8	4	
		4	1	6		7		3
				8	3	1	9	
		8	9	1		2		
	6	9	7		5			

Start with the center block, which needs 2,5, and 9. First find a space for the 9 that isn't in the same row or column as any other 9's. Then find where the 5 must go, and then put the 2 in the last empty place. Now find a place for a 3 in the middle column — and it can't be in the bottom block because there's already a 3 in there!

2

2						1	3	6
8				9	3	7		2
		8	5	3	4		2	7
	9	4			2			3
		2	6	1	9		8	5
3				7	8	2		4
4						8	6	9

You can start by putting all the 3's in! Remember, there should be one (and only one) 3 in every row, column, and 3x3 block. You can also put the missing 1 and 8 into the right-hand column and then complete the bottom right-hand block.

TRUFFLES' TIPS

3

	9	1				6	3	
			7		1			
5		6				7		8
	3		5		4		2	
		2				8		
	8		3		6		9	
8		3				5		9
			6		7			
	5	4				2	7	

8					3		7	4
	9		5		2	1		8
		3			7		9	
				3		9	4	1
	1				4			
6		7					5	
4		2	3			5		
5				1			2	
	3	1	4					7

5

	4		2		9		5	
	9			5			7	
	8						3	
		2	4	8	1	3		
8		1	5		3	4		7
				4				
9	1						8	5
5		6	7		8	9		3

Devious Puzzles

6

3							7	4
					3			
9		6		8			2	
	2			3	9			6
		9	7	6	5	8		
7				1	4		5	
	4				7		2	9
			6					
6	7							1

You can quickly finish the middle
block to start with, and you can also
put all the 7's in!

7

	7			4				
			6	2	5			
9		4	3	1				
5							2	
8				3		9	6	4
	4					7	3	
	3					2		
		1	9					8
2				5	3	1		

8

			3				6	
		5		7	2		4	
			1			7	2	
3					5			7
		1	6		8	3		
6			7					5
	5	3			9			
	2		5	1		4		
	4				3			

					5	6		
	8			6			2	
4			9					1
			3					2
6		2	4				1	
8	4	3		2	7	9		
		8	6	1				
7			5				4	
	5		2	7		8		

HARDER SU DOKUS

When you move onto harder Su Dokus, you might find that after you've put a few numbers into the grid, you get utterly and completely stuck. You get desperate hoping to find another number to put in, but there are so many possibilities to consider that your mind starts going around in circles and you end up trying out all the same ideas over and over again. In case you need a little more help, we have developed the handy portable "Calcatronic Su Doktor."

If you're too proud to ask a computer for help, our advice is to put the puzzle down and do something else, then come back to it. Then with a little luck you'll suddenly spot something you hadn't noticed before ... now get to it!

			3					
				1		7		
			6		7	3		2
4		5				8	9	
	2							6
		9			3		2	7
	6	7	2			5		4
			9		4			
		4		7	1	6		

TRUFFLES' TIPS

You can complete the bottom middle block right away. Put in the 6, then the 3, then the 5, and finally the 8.

								7
		2					6	
	7	9		6		3	4	2
5	3		2				8	4
	2				9			
7	9		8				1	3
	4	7		8		1	3	5
		1					2	
								8

13

6				3	5	9		
5	1		7	6			2	
1			8	5			9	
9	2				1	4	6	
		7			6	3		
			4					
				1		7		
			9	2	6	1		

2			8				3	
	1						5	
			4	6		9		
		3		8				1
7		5	1		2	4		9
9				7		2		
		4		5	3			
	6						2	
	3				8			5

9								
7		1	4					
		6			2	9		
1			2	7		4		
					4			
	3		9		1		6	
2	5					7	1	
	1	7	8					
		4			3		8	5

16

4			8	2	3			
			8	2	3			
9	5	8						
		9		8			7	
			5	6	4		9	
3	1			7			5	
2					7	3		
			9			5		
1		5	6			4		9

		8		6	1	7		
7	1	2					9	
		6					4	
8	9		5				6	
	5	3		7				
			6		3	9	7	
9			1	2		8		
	2			8		6		

	7		5		2		3	
8				7				9
	4						5	
			1		6			
		3				1		
4		2	7		3	9		6
		7				5		
	1	6	9		8	2	4	

					1		6	2
				2		9		
			4			1	8	
6	3			8	5			
7		4				5		6
			2	6			3	8
	9	3			2			
		8		9				
4	5		8					

1		2				6		
	5							
			5	7				2
8	1	4						
				4		3		
		3	9			5		
	3		6		2			8
9		7			5		2	
	4				7			3

Eeek! Professor Fiendish isn't too happy that Truffles has been giving tips, so he's just unveiled a nasty new invention ... It's two Su Dokus glued together, and the numbers in the middle box are the same for both of them. You have to treat it like two separate puzzles, but you'll need to solve them both at the same time.

The Dreaded Kjarposkos

The Wise Mathematicians at the Murderous Math Organization locked the door to the research lab, then they grabbed a pile of numbers and shapes and performed a series of dreadful experiments on them until suddenly...

Yes! At last they had created something with which they could frustrate the world, and just to make things worse, they gave it the most ridiculous name they could think of.

The KJARPOSKO involves a selection of boxes that are linked together. Each box is divided into two sections. There is a number on top, and you have to fill a number into the answer space underneath.

There's only one rule: *every number on top of a box equals the total of the answers in the bottom of the boxes linked to it.*

Confused? Don't panic — just look at these three boxes. You need to put the answers 1,2,3 into the spaces indicated by the letters a,b,c. The box with 4 in it is linked to the boxes with the spaces marked b and c. Therefore the numbers you put into b and c must add up to 4. In the same way a+b=5 and a+c=3.

When you fill a number into a space you can cross it off the list at the bottom. Here's the answer:

Now we'll try a harder one.

You have to fill the numbers 1-8 into the empty spaces. DON'T READ THE NEXT BIT if you think you're ready to solve this puzzle yourself! You can check your answer at the end of the book.

HOW TO SOLVE THIS PUZZLE
Fill in the numbers as you read these instructions

The 14 box is only connected to two others, so the answers in these two must be 6+8. (They can't be 7+7 as all answers are different.) Therefore the 8 box must have an answer of 6 or 8. The 15 box is only connected to two others, so these answers must be 7 + 8. Therefore the 8 box must contain the answer 8.

Immediately the 9 box must have the answer 7 (because 15=8+7) and the 10 box must have the answer 6 (because 14=8+6). Also the 6 box must have answer 5 (because 13=8+5).

The 9 box is connected to the 10 box, which already has the answer 6 in it. Therefore the other two boxes it is connected to must have the answers 1 and 2 (9=6+1+2). If answer 1 was in the 12 box, then there must be answer 5 in the 13 box (6=1+5). However we have already used the 5, so this is not possible. Therefore the answer 1 must be in the 15 box and the answer 2 in the 12 box.

Now the rest of the solution is obvious.

TRICKS

The hardest part of Kjarposkos is getting started. If you stare at a puzzle for long enough then eventually you'll realize where one number *has* to go. In the puzzle we just saw, we worked out that the 8 had to go in the 8 box. With harder puzzles this can be quite difficult, so you might prefer to try a few guesses. Before you guess, the secret is to find an empty box that only has a few possibilities. Here are a few tricks to try.

HIGHS AND LOWS

Find the box with the lowest number in it, then check the boxes it is connected to. For example, if a box has a 3 on top, you know that the two boxes connected to it can only have a 1 or 2 on the bottom. Examining the box with the highest number is also helpful, especially if it is only connected to two others. (We already did this by looking at both the 15 and 14 boxes in the puzzle we've already seen.)

SPLIT THE EVENS

Look for any box that has an even number in it and is only connected to two other boxes. The other two boxes *cannot* contain half of the even number. Eeek! This sounds complicated until you look at the diagram on the next page, which is a small part of a big puzzle. All we're saying is that 4 is an even number, so you can't put 2 in either the b space or d space. (If you put 2 in space b then you would have to put a 2 in space d because 2+2=4, but you cannot use the same number more than once.) So in this puzzle you would know that either b or d must be 1 and the other must be 3.

MAX AND MIN (this tip is quite advanced!)

In the diagram above, the 9 box tells us that a+c+d=9. You can make 9 from adding three different numbers in just three ways: 1+3+5 or 2+3+4 or 1+2+6. This tells us that none of a or c or d can be higher than 6.

Now look at the 16 box, which tells us a+b+e=16. The maximum possible value of a is 6, and the Split the Evens Tip showed us that the maximum of b is 3. Therefore the *minimum* possible value of e is 7.

If you experiment, you'll find that in this little section of puzzle, the only possible way you can fill in the spaces with no repeating numbers is: a=6 b=3 c=2 d=1 e=7.

If all else fails... GUESS! If you can't see where to start, put in one or two numbers with a pencil and see how they affect the rest of the puzzle. Even if you're wrong, this will help you find the right answer. Good Luck!

Kjarposko Puzzles

1

4	16	7
13		9
7	15	10

1 2 3 4 5 6 7 8

The 4 box tells you that the number in the 16 box must be 3 or 1. But if you try 1 you'll find that you can't finish the puzzle using all the numbers 1-8! Therefore the 3 goes in the 16 box. Remember – don't be scared to try out numbers with a pencil. You can always erase them if they don't work!

TRUFFLES' TIPS

2

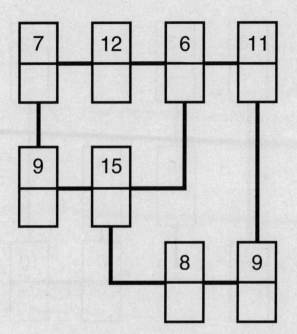

1 2 3 4 5 6 7 8

You can work out what should go in the bottom right 9 box. The 6 box has three connections, so the numbers you put in the boxes that they connect to must be 1+2+3. Since the 1, 2, and 3 are now used, the only combination of numbers the 15 box can be connected to are 4+5+6. This means that only numbers 7 and 8 remain to go in the bottom-right box, but if you try 8 then you can't put anything in the 15 box. Therefore what's the only number left...?

TRUFFLES' TIPS

3

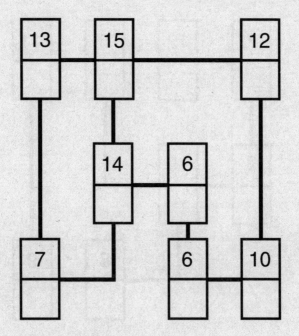

13   15   12

14   6

7   6   10

1 2 3 4 5 6 7 8

See the two 6 boxes? These have to be linked to 1+5 and 2+4. Now look at the 13 box. To get 13 you need 6+7 or 5+8, but the 5 has to be linked to a 6 box so it is not available. Therefore you can only make 13 with 6 +7. But the Split the Evens Tip tells you that the 6 cannot go in the 15 box...

4

1 2 3 4 5 6 7 8

THE FOUR BOX SHORTCUT!
Here's something to look out for when you see four
boxes linked in a ring and one of them isn't
linked to anything else. Look at the
11,17,12, and 13 boxes. The 11 box is only
linked to the 13 and 17 boxes, so we
know the answers in these boxes
must add up to 11. The 12 box is linked
to these same two boxes, but also to
the 14 box. Therefore the number in
the 14 box must be 12-11 = 1.

5

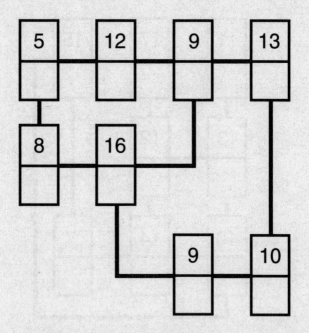

| 5 | 12 | 9 | 13 |

| 8 | 16 |

| 9 | 10 |

1 2 3 4 5 6 7 8

What goes in the 5 box? It's in-between 12 and 8, so it cannot be 4 or 6 because of the Split the Evens Tip. The 8 box means it cannot be 8, and if you try 1,2, or 3 then you can't put anything in the 9 box. Therefore the 5 box can only contain 5 or 7. Now try 7 with a pencil and see what happens...

TRUFFLES' TIPS

6

1 2 3 4 5 6 7 8

What is the only number that can go in the 14 box on the middle row? You might be able to do this in your head. Try all the numbers 1-8 and see how this affects the number in the 5 box. If you find a number that works, before you write it in, check what goes into the 8 box!

TRUFFLES' TIPS

WARNING!
Now that you've had some practice,
things are going to get much tougher.
Before continuing we suggest you fix
a smoke alarm to your head in case
your brain overheats.

7

1 2 3 4 5 6 7 8 9

The easiest place to start here is to
see what might go into the 19 box,
then fill in the 18, 17, and bottom 16
boxes. Then try to fill in the three
boxes connected to the 16 box at the
bottom with the unused numbers.

8

1 2 3 4 5 6 7 8 10

Here's something to watch out for. The 11 box must contain 9 or 10 (because of the 19 box). If you put 9 in the 11 box, then the numbers in the two 18 boxes must add up to 5 (because of the 14 box). However, the numbers in the central 18 box and the 19 box must also add up to 5 (because of the 5 box). This is called a CLASH! Suppose you put 1 in the central 18 box, then both the other 18 box and the 19 box will need a 4, which you can't do. In fact, you can't put anything in the 18 box and then fill in the other two boxes. Therefore ... the 11 box must contain the 10!

TRUFFLES' TIPS

9

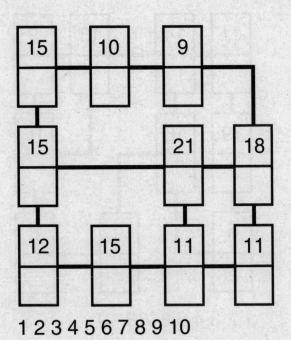

15	10	9	

15		21	18

12	15	11	11

1 2 3 4 5 6 7 8 9 10

You can use the Four Box Shortcut here!

TRUFFLES' TIPS

112

8   13   16   9

21   11

5   17   17   14

1 2 3 4 5 6 7 8 9 10

Just for practice — imagine putting 8 into the 17 box on the right. The 16 box then tells you that the numbers in the 13 box and 9 box must add to 8. However, the 8 box tells you that the numbers in the 13 box and 21 box also add to 8. It's a CLASH! Therefore you cannot put 8 into the right-hand 17 box.

TRUFFLES' TIPS

WARNING!
These puzzles are now becoming as difficult as drastic Kakuros!

PEEP PEEP PEEP

BRAIN TEMPERATURE: SIZZLING

11

```
        ┌─────┬─────┐
        │  8  │ 17  │
        ├─────┤     │
  ┌─────┼─────┼─────┼─────┐
  │  5  │ 20  │ 14  │ 25  │
  ├─────┼─────┼─────┼─────┤
  │ 18  │  6  │ 22  │ 10  │
  ├─────┼─────┼─────┼─────┤
        │ 22  │ 14  │
        └─────┴─────┘
```

1 2 3 4 5 6 7 8 9 10 11 12

TRUFFLES' TIPS

You can use the Four Box Shortcut here! If you can find it, you'll see what number has to go in the 22 box.

114

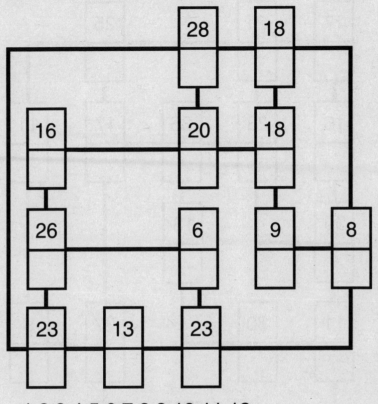

28 18

16 20 18

26 6 9 8

23 13 23

1 2 3 4 5 6 7 8 9 10 11 12

Once again, the Four Box Shortcut might save your brain here, and don't forget to look for more Four Box Shortcuts in the later puzzles. Sorry, this is the last tip I can give you! From now on you're ON YOUR OWN!

TRUFFLES' TIPS

13

1 2 3 4 5 6 7 8 9 10
11 12 13 14 15 16

1 2 3 4 5 6 7 8 9 10
11 12 13 14 15 16

WARNING!
These puzzles are now DANGEROUS!
Proceed with extreme caution.

BRAIN TEMPERATURE: CRITICAL

1 2 3 4 5 6 7 8 9 10 11
12 13 14 15 16 17 18

16

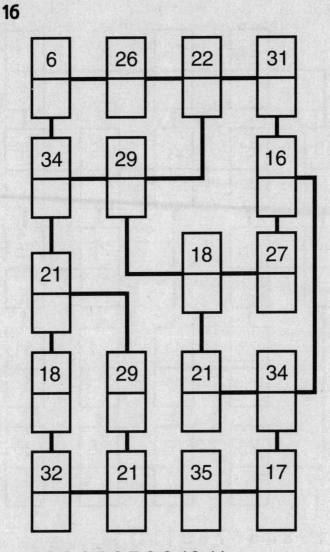

1 2 3 4 5 6 7 8 9 10 11
12 13 14 15 16 17 18

17

1 2 3 4 5 6 7 8 9 10 11 12
13 14 15 16 17 18 19 20

18

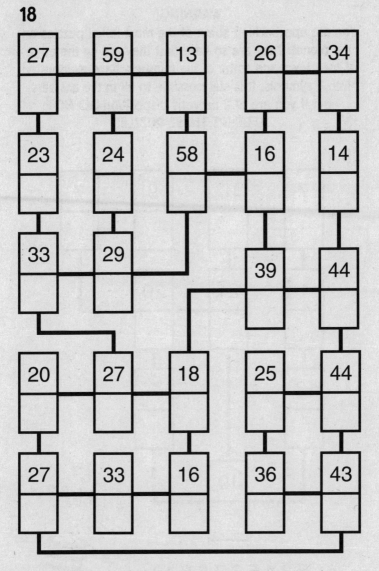

1 2 3 4 5 6 7 8 9 10 11 12 13 14
15 16 17 18 19 20 21 22 23 24

121

19

1 2 3 4 5 6 7 8 9 10

1 2 3 4 5 6 7 8 9 10 12

1 2 3 4 5 6 7 8 9 10 11 12 13

There! That's the last of the Kjarposkos. If you managed to complete them all then CONGRATULATIONS! You have won a Star Prize from Pongo McWhiffy's Delux Burger bar... but you'll never guess what mystery flavor it is!

Solutions

KAKURO PUZZLES

1

```
9 8 . 2 1 4 . 2 4 1 . 5 9
7 9 8 6 3 5 . 6 5 3 9 8 7
. 7 9 . . 1 2 3 . . 7 9 .
2 1 . . . 2 4 1 . . 6 2 .
1 3 . . 2 6 . 4 3 . 3 1 .
4 2 5 9 1 3 . 5 1 2 3 7 4
. . 9 8 . . . . . 1 5 . .
2 4 6 7 9 8 . 6 7 8 9 5 4
1 6 . . 7 9 . 5 9 . 6 2 .
4 8 . . 6 4 1 . . . 3 1 .
. 9 8 . . 1 2 3 . . 9 8 .
8 7 9 1 3 2 . 2 1 3 7 9 8
9 5 . 2 1 4 . 4 2 1 . 7 9
```

2

```
1 5 8 . 2 1 . . 2 1 . . .
3 7 9 . 4 3 5 . 1 3 4 . .
. 3 6 2 1 . 2 1 3 . 1 2 4
7 9 . 1 3 . 1 3 . . 7 8 9
9 8 5 6 . 1 3 . 6 8 2 9 7
. 1 3 2 4 . . 7 9 . . 4 6
6 4 2 . 1 3 . 7 9 . 6 1 8
9 2 . 1 3 . . 6 8 9 7 . .
1 3 8 2 4 . 2 9 . 8 9 6 7
2 1 3 . . 2 1 . 2 1 . 8 9
8 6 9 . 2 1 3 . 1 3 2 5 .
. 4 2 1 . 5 2 4 . 1 7 3 .
. . 1 3 . . 1 3 . 3 9 8 .
```

3

```
. 2 1 . . 1 3 2 . . 1 5 .
1 3 5 2 . 2 1 4 . 7 3 4 2
2 1 . 6 9 8 . 7 9 8 . 1 3
4 5 8 9 7 6 . 9 8 6 7 2 1
. . 9 5 . 7 9 8 . 9 8 . .
9 6 7 8 . 9 8 6 . 5 9 8 7
7 9 . . . . . . . . 9 8 .
6 8 9 7 . 4 1 2 . 8 7 5 9
. . 8 9 . 2 3 1 . 9 8 . .
2 1 6 8 7 9 . 6 8 5 9 2 1
1 3 . 6 9 8 . 8 9 7 . 1 3
4 2 1 5 . 5 9 7 . 6 3 4 2
. 4 3 . . 7 6 9 . . 1 5 .
```

4

```
9 8 . . 8 4 . 2 1 . . 2 1
7 9 8 . 6 2 1 5 3 . 2 1 3
. 7 9 8 . 3 2 1 . 5 1 3 .
. . 3 5 6 1 . 6 1 2 3 . .
2 6 . 9 8 6 . 7 3 1 . 5 1
4 8 6 7 9 5 . 8 5 4 9 7 3
. 9 8 . . . . . . . 8 9 .
3 7 9 5 8 4 . 7 9 4 6 8 3
1 5 . 3 7 1 . 1 5 2 . 6 1
. . 3 1 6 2 . 3 8 1 2 . .
. 3 1 2 . 3 1 2 . 3 1 2 .
3 1 2 . 1 5 2 4 3 . 3 1 2
1 2 . . 3 6 . 5 1 . . 3 1
```

5

```
. 9 8 . 2 1 8 6 9 . 2 1 3
4 6 1 . 1 3 9 8 7 . 4 2 1
9 8 2 7 3 . 7 9 . 9 1 . .
. . 6 9 8 . 5 7 9 8 . 7 9
3 1 . 6 9 8 . 3 5 7 9 8 .
1 2 8 5 . 7 9 . 7 9 8 6 .
. 3 5 . 9 8 5 . 8 6 . . .
8 9 7 5 . 7 9 . 2 5 3 1 .
6 8 9 1 3 . 2 3 1 . 4 2 .
9 7 . 2 1 8 6 . 9 8 6 . .
. 1 3 . 1 3 . 7 4 3 8 9 .
2 1 4 . 3 7 9 1 8 . 9 6 8
1 3 2 . 1 9 8 2 6 . 7 9 .
```

6

```
. 3 1 . 9 7 . 9 7 . 3 1 .
. 9 7 8 5 6 . 5 6 8 9 7 .
. 8 9 6 . 9 5 8 . 6 8 9 .
. 1 2 . 8 9 7 . . 1 2 . .
. 7 3 4 2 . . 6 5 7 3 . .
. . 1 3 2 . 1 4 2 . . . .
. . 2 1 4 . 3 2 1 . . . .
. 6 8 3 5 . . 1 3 6 8 . .
. 2 1 . 7 6 9 . . 2 1 . .
. 9 7 8 . 9 8 6 . 8 9 7 .
. 8 9 6 7 5 . 5 7 6 8 9 .
. 1 3 . 9 8 . 8 9 . 1 3 .
```

125

7

9	8	4	6	7		4	1	3	2	6
7	9	6	8	5		5	2	1	6	8
3	1			8	9	6			7	9
2	4	1		9	7	8		2	1	4
1	6	3	4				2	1	3	7
			9	8		9	8			
			7	9		7	9			
6	1	3	2				7	8	6	9
4	2	1		8	9	6		9	3	7
1	3			9	7	8			1	3
9	7	8	5	6		3	8	1	2	4
8	9	6	7	4		7	9	3	4	8

8

4	2			9	7		9	7		4	2
9	7	8	5	6		5	6	8	9	7	
8	9	6		8	9	6		6	8	9	
2	1			2	4	1			2	1	
1	3		6	9	7	8	4		1	3	
	1	3				1	3				
	2	1				2	1				
6	8		2	3	9	7	5		6	8	
1	3			1	6	3			1	3	
9	7	8		6	8	9		8	9	7	
8	9	6	7	5		5	7	6	8	9	
2	1		9	8		8	9		2	1	

9

8	4	3	9		8	9			8	9
4	2	1	7		9	7	8		9	7
3	1		8	7			9	7	6	8
9	6	8		9	5	8		9	5	
7	3	5	9		9	7	2		1	3
		7	8	9		3	1	5	2	4
9	8	1	2	6		9	6	8		
7	9		1	3	2		4	9	3	7
	4	3		5	1	2		3	1	2
4	2	1	3		1	2		7	2	6
1	3		6	8	9		1	7	2	6
2	1			9	7		3	9	6	8

10

	9	4	5		9	8		7	9	
9	8	1	3		4	6	5	9	8	7
5	7	2	1	4		7	9		5	9
		7	9	8	6	5		9	7	
3	1	5		7	9		1	3		
1	2			9	8		2	4	3	1
2	4	3	1		7	4			1	2
	1	2		3	1		1	2	4	
	8	2		4	5	2	1	3		
9	5		9	7		6	9	8	4	3
8	7	9	5	6	4		7	9	2	1
	9	8		8	9		5	6	1	

11

9	8		7	9			9	8		
7	9		6	8	9		7	6	8	
8	6	7	9		8	7		7	9	
		6	8	9		8	7	9	6	
	7	9		7	8	5	9			
7	9	8	6		7	9		7	9	
9	8		5	9		6	7	9	8	
	9	8	7	6		9	8			
8	6	7	9		7	9	8			
9	7		7	8		7	6	9	8	
6	9	7		9	7	6		8	6	
	8	9			9	8		7	9	

12

	3	1				3	4		
5	1	2	3		3	1	2	5	
7	9		2	6	8	1		1	7
9	8	7		8	9		8	7	9
8	6	9		9	7		6	9	8
	6	7			8	9			
	8	9			9	7			
1	2	3		9	7		1	4	2
2	4	1		8	9		3	2	1
3	1		5	6	8	9		1	3
5	9	8	7			7	8	9	5
	7	9				9	7		

13

	3	1				3	4		
5	1	2	3		3	1	2	7	
7	9		2	6	8	1		1	5
9	8	7		8	9		8	7	9
8	6	9		9	7		6	9	8
	6	7			9	7			
	8	9			8	9			
1	2	3		7	9		1	4	2
2	4	1		9	8		3	2	1
3	1		7	8	6	9		1	3
5	6	8	9			7	8	9	4
	7	9				9	7		

14

	5	1		2	1		7	5	
2	4	3		1	3		8	9	6
1	3		1	4	2	8		7	9
4	1	3	2			9	7	6	8
	2	1					9	8	
		4	3		9	5			
		2	1		7	6			
	5	9				1	8		
2	4	7	1		7	8	9	6	
1	3		7	8	6	9		7	9
4	1	3		7	9		7	6	8
	2	1		9	8		9	5	

15

9	6	8					1	2	3
1	2	9	3			8	3	6	9
3	1		8	7	9	6		1	5
	3	8			9	8		1	3
		7	9				7	9	
		9	8				9	8	
	8	6			7	9		3	2
1	3		7	9	8	6		7	9
2	6	1	3			7	9	4	8
3	9	5					5	1	7

16

1	3			1	3		3	2	1
6	8		1	2	4		1	4	2
9	7	8	6		2	1		5	3
8	9	6			4	1	3	2	6
2	1		3	1		5	1		
		1	5		1	2		7	3
	7	3	2	1	4		8	9	7
1	3			1	3	7	6	8	9
2	8	1		4	3	9		3	1
4	9	6			2	1		1	2

17

6	9	8					9	6	8
2	1	9	3			3	7	1	2
1	3		5	1	2	4		4	9
	2	4			3	1		3	2
		1	2				1	2	
		3	1				3	1	
	7	9			1	2		4	2
1	3		6	3	1	9		7	9
4	9	6	8			7	9	3	8
2	8	1					4	1	6

18

		2	1			7	9		
4	2	1	3			9	8	3	7
1	3		5	7	9	8		1	3
2	1	5		9	8		8	6	9
	8	9	7			8	7	9	
	6	8	9			6	9	8	
8	5	7		7	9		5	2	1
9	7		7	9	8	2		5	3
6	9	7	8			3	1	4	2
	9	5				1	2		

19

	5	9		4	3		6	9	8
9	8	7		5	1	6	8	7	9
7	9		1	3			7	9	
	6	4	2	1	3		7	2	4
	9	4	2	1	3			3	1
2	4	1			2	1		1	2
3	1		9	8			2	5	3
1	2		5	7	1	2	3		
5	3	9		9	2	4	1	8	
	5	9		3	1			9	8
8	9	6	7	1	5		8	7	9
9	7	8		3	4		9	5	

20

9	8	7	5			1	3	8	9
8	6	9	7			2	1	9	7
7	9		4	1	2	3		6	8
5	7	8		3	1		9	7	5
	1	2				1	2		
	3	1				3	1		
7	5	9		1	2		4	3	5
6	8		4	3	1	2		1	3
9	7	8	5			3	1	4	2
8	9	6	7			5	3	2	1

21

		7	9			9	8		
7	6	9	8			7	9	6	8
9	8		5	9	7	8		7	9
	2	5	4	8	9	6	3	1	
8	7	9				1	2	3	
6	9	8				2	4	1	
	1	7	2	5	8	6	4	9	
1	3		5	7	9	8		3	1
2	4	1	3			9	8	5	2
	2	1				7	9		

22

2	3	6	1		1	2		2	1
4	5	9	2		3	6	8	7	9
	7	8	4	9	6		6	9	8
7	9			7	2	9		1	3
9	8	7	6	5		7	9		
		9	8		5	6	8	9	7
2	5		9	2	7			8	9
8	9	7		6	9	8	4	7	
6	8	9	7	3		6	1	3	2
9	7		2	1		9	2	5	4

23

8	9	7		9	8		9	8	6
6	8	9			7	9		7	9	8
9	7		9	8	6	7		7	9
1	6	2	3			6	9	5	7
		5	1			8	5		
		1	2			3	7		
5	7	9	8			9	8	7	5
8	6		6	4	2	5		9	7
9	8	6		2	1		9	6	8
7	9	8		1	3		7	8	9

24

	5	3	1	2		1	3	8	9
3	7	1	2	4		2	1	9	7
8	9		3	1	2	4		2	1
		6	4		1	3		7	2
	4	8		2	4		7	6	
	7	9		1	3		9	5	
3	5		1	3		4	8		
1	3		2	4	1	3		1	3
2	1	3	4		2	1	3	5	4
4	2	5	9		4	2	1	3	

25

1	2	4		4	7	9		1	3
3	1	5	9	6	8	7		2	1
		9	8	7			8	5	
7	5	8		1	2		9	7	5
8	9		2	9	7	1		8	9
9	7		1	8	9	3		9	7
6	8	9		3	1		3	6	8
	6	7			3	2	1		
1	2		9	7	4	1	5	2	3
3	1		8	9	6		2	4	1

26

1	3		6	9	8		9	8	7		1	3
2	1	6	8	7	9		5	9	6	8	2	1
	8	9		5	8	6		8	9			
	9	7		7	9	8		9	7			
3	1		8	4		4	8			3	1	
4	5	1	3	6	2		2	6	3	1	4	5
	2	1	4			4	1	2				
1	3	4	2	9	8		8	9	2	4	1	3
2	1		7	9		9	7		2	1		
	9	8		4	3	1		9	8			
	7	9		2	1	4		7	9			
1	2	8	6	9	7		7	9	8	6	1	2
3	1		3	7	5		5	8	6		3	1

27

9	7		5	9		8	9		4	5	9
6	3	9	8	7		9	7		9	1	3	7
2	1	7	9		9	7		9	7	2	1	4
	3	1	2	4		8	5		4	8		
8	6	5		1	3	2		6	8	5		
9	7		9	3		8	9		9	8		
6	9	7	8		8	9	7		8	7	9	6
	8	9		9	7		9	7		7	9	
	8	5	1		6	9	7		9	6	8	
6	2		2	3		8	6	9	7			
7	3	9	1	2		8	7		1	3	8	9
9	6	8	3		8	9		3	2	1	4	7
5	1	6		9	7		1	5		1	3	

28

3	7	9	1	8		3	1	9	8	7
1	9	8	2	6		1	2	8	6	9
	1	6		7	9	8		7	9	
1	2	7		9	8	6		5	3	1
3	4		2	5		2	3		7	2
		1	3			1	3			
		2	1			2	1			
3	4		9	5		3	4		3	1
1	2	6		7	9	8		5	4	2
	1	3		9	8	6		7	9	
3	7	9	1	8		2	1	8	6	9
1	9	8	2	6		1	3	9	8	7

29

	9	6	8		7	9		5	8
9	8	3	1		6	8	5	9	7
7	6	1	2	3	4		6	8	9
		2	4	1		3	1	6	2
	6	5	7		4	1	2		
7	9		6	7	9		7	9	
9	8		9	8	7		9	8	
	8	9	6		6	8	5		
4	8	9	7		2	3	5		
2	1	4		7	6	8	9	4	3
1	3	5	2	4		9	7	2	1
5	2		1	3		2	4	1	

30

	5	7		9	7		5	8	7	9
5	8	9	7	6	2		7	6	9	8
9	7		9	8		8	9		1	2
	9	7		5	9	7		3	1	
1	4	9	7		8	9	7		8	6
3	6	8	9	7		1	2	6		
	2	4	1		6	4	9	7	1	
6	8		8	3	1		6	8	9	3
2	1		2	5	4		1	3		
1	3		1	4		1	2		8	9
8	9	6	7		2	3	1	4	6	7
9	7	1	2		1	5		2	1	

31

```
5 7 . 8 3 . . 4 2 1 3
8 6 . 9 7 8 . 2 1 3 5
7 9 8 4 1 6 . 1 3 . .
9 8 6 . . 5 4 7 9 8 6
. 4 8 6 9 7 . 7 9 8 .
5 7 . 6 9 . 8 9 . 7 9
7 9 . 9 7 . 9 7 . 5 7
9 8 7 . 8 9 6 5 3 . .
8 6 9 4 5 7 . . 9 8 6
. 1 3 . 6 1 4 7 9 8 .
5 3 2 1 . 8 7 9 . 7 9
9 1 4 2 . . 3 8 . 5 7
```

32

```
3 1 2 9 7 . 3 2 1 9 7
1 2 4 8 9 . 1 4 2 8 9
9 7 . 6 8 9 . . 3 1 .
8 9 . 8 9 7 . . 1 2 .
. 1 2 4 . . 4 1 2 . .
2 1 9 7 . . 8 9 6 7 .
1 3 8 9 . . 9 7 8 5 .
. 3 1 4 . 2 3 1 . . .
8 9 . 6 8 9 . . 1 2 .
9 7 . 8 9 7 . . 3 1 .
3 1 2 9 7 . 3 2 1 9 7
1 2 4 8 9 . 1 4 2 8 9
```

33

```
. 4 9 . 3 4 . 3 1 . 3 1
9 6 8 . 1 2 . 1 2 . 9 4 6
7 1 4 2 . 5 4 9 . 4 6 2 1
. . 6 1 . 3 1 2 . 9 8 .
. 2 1 . . 1 2 4 . . 2 9
4 1 3 5 2 6 . 5 8 6 1 4 2
1 3 . . 3 1 . . 7 9 . 3 1
2 4 7 9 8 6 . 5 9 8 6 1 4
. 5 9 . . 5 4 9 . . 4 2
. . 3 9 . 3 1 2 . 1 2 .
3 9 5 8 . 1 2 4 . 3 1 2 9
1 3 2 . 3 4 . 3 1 . 9 6 8
. 5 1 . 1 2 . 1 2 . 3 1
```

34

```
. 1 2 . 8 4 . 1 4 2
6 4 9 . 6 3 . 3 2 1
1 2 8 5 9 7 . . 1 3
. . 7 9 . 2 1 9 3 5
8 9 6 . . 6 9 8 . .
3 7 1 8 . 1 3 . 8 7
9 6 . 6 1 . 7 8 9 5
. . 1 4 2 . . 4 2 1
5 7 3 9 6 . 1 3 . .
8 6 . . 4 3 5 2 1 9
9 8 6 . 7 2 . 6 9 8
7 9 8 . 5 1 . 1 3 .
```

35

```
. 8 6 9 3 . 6 3 9 8 .
. 6 2 7 1 . 3 1 7 9 .
. 9 7 . 4 1 2 . 3 1 .
2 4 1 . 2 3 1 . 2 4 1
1 7 3 2 . . 4 1 6 3 .
. . 4 8 1 3 2 . . . .
. . 5 9 2 1 6 . . . .
7 9 4 8 . . 5 6 1 3 .
9 8 6 . 2 4 1 . 4 2 1
. 7 9 . 1 2 3 . 1 3 .
. 3 1 9 7 . 6 1 9 7 .
. 1 2 7 4 . 2 3 8 9 .
```

36

```
1 2 3 5 . 2 1 . . .
2 4 1 3 . 5 3 1 2 4
3 1 . 7 9 . 5 3 1 2
9 7 . 4 7 9 2 . 3 1
. . 2 1 3 7 . 7 9 .
9 8 4 2 1 . . 1 5 3
3 5 1 . . 1 2 4 8 9
. 9 7 . 7 3 1 2 . .
1 3 . 8 9 7 4 . 3 5
2 1 3 7 . 9 7 . 1 3
4 2 1 5 3 . 3 1 4 2
. . 9 7 . 5 3 2 1 .
```

37

4	9	7		9	8		7	9		7	9	4
2	5	1	3	7	4		6	5	7	9	8	2
1	8	9	6		9	6	8		6	5	3	1
	3	2		5	7	8	9	6		8	6	
9	7		4	1	2		1	2	4		7	9
8	6	9	7	3	1		3	1	6	4	5	8
		8	9				8	7				
8	5	6	3	7	1		3	1	7	9	4	2
9	7		8	9	7		8	2	9		3	1
	3	5		5	2	3	1	4		2	8	
7	2	1	4		4	1	2		3	1	2	8
9	4	6	8	7	5		6	8	4	5	7	9
8	1	3		9	8		7	9		3	1	6

38

	7	9		9	5		5	1		5	7	
9	3	5		7	6		4	3		7	9	1
8	1	2	3		8	9	6		7	9	8	3
	2	4	1		1	4	2		9	8	6	
3	4			5	9	7	1	2			3	1
1	5	6	2	3	7		3	8	9	6	5	2
		8	9	6				4	2	1		
8	5	2	4	1	3		2	1	4	3	6	7
9	7			2	5	6	1	3			5	9
	6	8	9		9	8	6		9	6	8	
2	8	9	7		7	9	8		7	8	9	3
1	9	7		7	6		7	9		9	7	1
	1	2		9	8		9	8		1	2	

39

8	6	9				1	2	4
2	1	6	4		8	2	9	7
1	3	8	9		6	4	8	9
9	2		8	7	9	5		4	6
6	4	8		9	8		2	1	8
		7	9			7	9		
		9	8			9	8		
1	8	2		7	9		7	6	4
4	6		3	9	8	2		8	1
9	7	2	1			1	2	7	9
8	9	4	6			6	4	9	8
2	4	1				1	4	2

40

		8	6	9	7	4		7	5
	3	1	4	8	9	2		9	7
3	1	2		5	2	1	9	6	8
2	6		4	7	3		7	8	9
	4	1	2		6	7			
1	2	3	5		8	9		7	9
3	5		3	4		6	7	9	8
		1	2		8	9	6		
1	2	3		7	3	5		1	2
2	4	1	9	8	5		1	3	4
3	1		6	3	1	4	2	5	
8	9		8	1	2	6	9		

BRIDGE PUZZLES

Here is how the starting puzzle on page 54 should look when you've finished:

130

1

2

3

4

5

6

7

8

9

10

11

12

13

14

15

16

17

18

19

20

133

SU DOKU PUZZLES

1

9	4	1	8	3	6	5	7	2
6	7	3	5	9	2	4	1	8
8	5	2	4	7	1	9	3	6
3	1	7	2	4	8	6	5	9
2	9	6	3	5	7	8	4	1
5	8	4	1	6	9	7	2	3
4	2	5	6	8	3	1	9	7
7	3	8	9	1	4	2	6	5
1	6	9	7	2	5	3	8	4

2

1	4	3	2	6	7	5	9	8
2	7	9	8	4	5	1	3	6
8	5	6	1	9	3	7	4	2
6	1	8	5	3	4	9	2	7
5	9	4	7	8	2	6	1	3
7	3	2	6	1	9	4	8	5
3	6	1	9	7	8	2	5	4
4	2	7	3	5	1	8	6	9
9	8	5	4	2	6	3	7	1

3

7	9	1	8	4	5	6	3	2
3	2	8	7	6	1	9	4	5
5	4	6	2	9	3	7	1	8
9	3	7	5	8	4	1	2	6
4	6	2	1	7	9	8	5	3
1	8	5	3	2	6	4	9	7
8	7	3	4	1	2	5	6	9
2	1	9	6	5	7	3	8	4
6	5	4	9	3	8	2	7	1

4

8	5	6	1	9	3	2	7	4
7	9	4	5	6	2	1	3	8
1	2	3	8	4	7	6	9	5
2	8	5	7	3	6	9	4	1
3	1	9	2	5	4	7	8	6
6	4	7	9	8	1	3	5	2
4	6	2	3	7	8	5	1	9
5	7	8	6	1	9	4	2	3
9	3	1	4	2	5	8	6	7

5

6	4	7	2	3	9	8	5	1
1	9	3	8	5	6	2	7	4
2	8	5	1	7	4	6	3	9
7	5	2	4	8	1	3	9	6
4	3	9	6	2	7	5	1	8
8	6	1	5	9	3	4	2	7
3	7	8	9	4	5	1	6	2
9	1	4	3	6	2	7	8	5
5	2	6	7	1	8	9	4	3

6

3	8	2	5	9	6	1	7	4
4	5	7	2	1	3	6	9	8
9	1	6	4	8	7	3	2	5
5	2	4	8	3	9	7	1	6
1	3	9	7	6	5	8	4	2
7	6	8	1	4	2	9	5	3
8	4	5	3	7	1	2	6	9
2	9	1	6	5	8	4	3	7
6	7	3	9	2	4	5	8	1

7

6	7	2	8	4	9	5	1	3
3	1	8	6	2	5	4	9	7
9	5	4	3	1	7	6	8	2
5	9	3	7	6	4	8	2	1
8	2	7	5	3	1	9	6	4
1	4	6	2	9	8	7	3	5
7	3	5	1	8	6	2	4	9
4	6	1	9	7	2	3	5	8
2	8	9	4	5	3	1	7	6

8

2	1	7	3	9	4	5	6	8
9	6	5	8	7	2	1	4	3
4	3	8	1	5	6	7	2	9
3	8	2	9	4	5	6	1	7
5	7	1	6	2	8	3	9	4
6	9	4	7	3	1	2	8	5
1	5	3	4	6	9	8	7	2
8	2	9	5	1	7	4	3	6
7	4	6	2	8	3	9	5	1

9

2	1	7	8	4	5	6	3	9
3	8	9	7	6	1	5	2	4
4	6	5	9	3	2	7	8	1
5	9	1	3	8	6	4	7	2
6	7	2	4	5	9	3	1	8
8	4	3	1	2	7	9	6	5
9	3	8	6	1	4	2	5	7
7	2	6	5	9	8	1	4	3
1	5	4	2	7	3	8	9	6

10

3	6	9	8	1	7	4	2	5
4	1	8	5	6	2	7	3	9
5	2	7	3	4	9	6	1	8
1	4	5	7	9	3	2	8	6
7	8	6	1	2	5	3	9	4
9	3	2	4	8	6	1	5	7
8	5	4	6	3	1	9	7	2
2	7	1	9	5	4	8	6	3
6	9	3	2	7	8	5	4	1

11

7	4	2	3	8	5	9	6	1
3	9	6	4	1	2	7	8	5
1	5	8	6	9	7	3	4	2
4	7	5	1	2	6	8	9	3
8	2	3	7	4	9	1	5	6
6	1	9	8	5	3	4	2	7
9	6	7	2	3	8	5	1	4
5	3	1	9	6	4	2	7	8
2	8	4	5	7	1	6	3	9

12

6	1	3	4	2	8	5	9	7
4	5	2	7	9	3	8	6	1
8	7	9	1	6	5	3	4	2
5	3	6	2	1	7	9	8	4
1	2	8	3	4	9	7	5	6
7	9	4	8	5	6	2	1	3
9	4	7	6	8	2	1	3	5
3	8	1	5	7	4	6	2	9
2	6	5	9	3	1	4	7	8

13

3	7	9	2	4	8	1	5	6
6	8	2	1	3	5	9	7	4
5	1	4	7	6	9	8	2	3
1	3	6	8	5	4	2	9	7
9	2	8	3	7	1	4	6	5
4	5	7	9	2	6	3	8	1
2	6	1	4	8	7	5	3	9
8	9	5	6	1	3	7	4	2
7	4	3	5	9	2	6	1	8

14

2	9	7	8	1	5	6	3	4
4	1	6	3	2	9	8	5	7
3	5	8	4	6	7	9	1	2
6	2	3	9	8	4	5	7	1
7	8	5	1	3	2	4	6	9
9	4	1	5	7	6	2	8	3
8	7	4	2	5	3	1	9	6
5	6	9	7	4	1	3	2	8
1	3	2	6	9	8	7	4	5

15

9	2	3	5	8	7	1	4	6
7	8	1	4	9	6	3	5	2
5	4	6	1	3	2	9	7	8
1	6	5	2	7	8	4	3	9
8	7	9	3	6	4	5	2	1
4	3	2	9	5	1	8	6	7
2	5	8	6	4	9	7	1	3
3	1	7	8	2	5	6	9	4
6	9	4	7	1	3	2	8	5

16

4	3	2	7	9	5	6	8	1
7	6	1	8	2	3	9	4	5
9	5	8	4	1	6	7	3	2
5	4	9	3	8	1	2	7	6
8	2	7	5	6	4	1	9	3
3	1	6	2	7	9	8	5	4
2	9	4	1	5	7	3	6	8
6	8	3	9	4	2	5	1	7
1	7	5	6	3	8	4	2	9

17

6	3	9	2	4	7	1	5	8
5	4	8	9	6	1	7	2	3
7	1	2	8	3	5	4	9	6
2	7	6	3	9	8	5	4	1
8	9	4	5	1	2	3	6	7
1	5	3	4	7	6	2	8	9
4	8	1	6	5	3	9	7	2
9	6	7	1	2	4	8	3	5
3	2	5	7	8	9	6	1	4

18

6	7	9	5	4	2	8	3	1
1	2	4	8	3	9	7	6	5
8	3	5	6	7	1	4	2	9
2	4	1	3	9	7	6	5	8
5	9	8	1	2	6	3	7	4
7	6	3	4	8	5	1	9	2
4	5	2	7	1	3	9	8	6
9	8	7	2	6	4	5	1	3
3	1	6	9	5	8	2	4	7

19

8	4	7	9	5	1	3	6	2
5	6	1	3	2	8	9	7	4
3	2	9	4	7	6	1	8	5
6	3	2	7	8	5	4	1	9
7	8	4	1	3	9	5	2	6
9	1	5	2	6	4	7	3	8
1	9	3	6	4	2	8	5	7
2	7	8	5	9	3	6	4	1
4	5	6	8	1	7	2	9	3

20

1	7	2	3	8	4	6	9	5
4	5	9	1	2	6	8	3	7
3	6	8	5	7	9	4	1	2
8	1	4	7	5	3	2	6	9
6	9	5	2	4	8	3	7	1
7	2	3	9	6	1	5	8	4
5	3	1	6	9	2	7	4	8
9	8	7	4	3	5	1	2	6
2	4	6	8	1	7	9	5	3

Page 98

5	4	9	7	3	1	2	8	6						
6	7	8	9	2	5	3	1	4						
2	3	1	8	4	6	5	9	7						
7	9	2	5	1	4	6	3	8						
8	5	6	3	9	7	4	2	1						
4	1	3	2	6	8	9	7	5						
1	2	5	4	8	3	7	6	9	5	2	1	8	3	4
3	8	7	6	5	9	1	4	2	3	8	9	5	6	7
9	6	4	1	7	2	8	5	3	6	4	7	2	1	9
						5	2	7	8	1	3	4	9	6
						9	3	8	2	6	4	7	5	1
						6	1	4	9	7	5	3	2	8
						3	8	5	4	9	6	1	7	2
						2	7	6	1	3	8	9	4	5
						4	9	1	7	5	2	6	8	3

136

KJARPOSKO PUZZLES

This is how the test puzzle should look when it's finished:

1

2

3

4

5

| 5 | 12 | 9 | 13 |
| 5 | 4 | 7 | 2 |

| 8 | 16 | | |
| 1 | 3 | | |

| | | 9 | 10 |
| | | 8 | 6 |

6

| 5 | 14 | | |
| 6 | 2 | | |

| 12 | 12 | 14 | 12 |
| 3 | 5 | 8 | 7 |

| | 12 | | 8 |
| | 1 | | 4 |

7

6	19	5
5	4	8
18	16	17
2	6	1
11	16	10
7	9	3

8

11	14	18	9
10	7	3	5
19	18		16
4	1		6
5		9	8
9		2	8

9

15	10	9	
1	5	9	
15		21	18
10		6	4
12	15	11	11
8	2	7	3

10

8	13	16	9
7	6	4	1
21			11
2			5
5	17	17	14
8	3	9	10

11

12

13

14

15

16

17

18

19

7	18	9	7
8	5	1	4
*	21	20	
2	9	6	
12		*	
3		7	
	19		
	10		

20

20	16	11	12
4	8	10	3
*			17
12			2
26		14	11
7		9	6
18	*		20
11	5		1

21

*	*	33	16
9	13	4	8
15			22
5			12
*	40		21
6	7		10
17	11	*	11
3	11	1	2

Even if you got all the puzzles right, did you guess the flavor of your Prize Burger?